Verklärte Nacht and Pierrot Lunaire

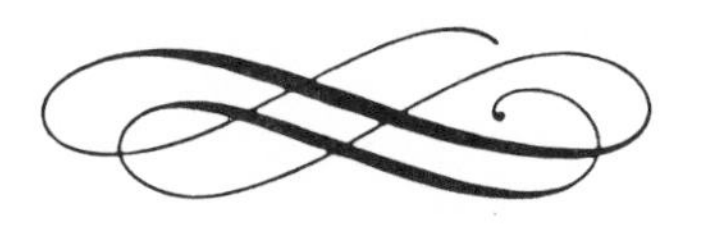

ARNOLD SCHOENBERG

Dover Publications, Inc.
NEW YORK

Copyright

Bibliographical Note

This Dover edition, first published in 1994, is a republication in one volume of two works originally published by Universal Edition: *Verklärte Nacht*, Op. 4, 1899; and *Pierrot lunaire*, Op. 21, 1914. The Dover edition adds: an overall contents page; an English translation of the original contents page for *Pierrot*, including the shifting instrumentation (corrected) of the twenty-one pieces in this work, introduced by a new editorial note; a glossary of German terms used in both scores, including translations of footnotes and longer score notes; and new English translations by Stanley Appelbaum of both Schoenberg's foreword to *Pierrot* and the poems on which the two works are based. Performance instructions for connecting the pieces in *Pierrot* are translated in the score.

Library of Congress Cataloging-in-Publication Data

Schoenberg, Arnold, 1874–1951.
[Verklärte Nacht]
Verklärte Nacht ; and, Pierrot lunaire / Arnold Schoenberg.
p. cm.
The 1st work for 2 violins, 2 violas, and 2 violoncellos; based on the poem Weib und Welt by Richard Dehmel; 2nd work for voice (Sprechstimme), piano, flute/piccolo, clarinet/bass clarinet, violin/viola, and violoncello; poems by Albert Giraud, German translations by Otto Erich Hartleben.
Reprint. Originally published: Universal Edition, 1899 (1st work, op. 4) and 1914 (2nd work, op. 21).
Includes a new editorial note, a glossary of German terms, and new English translations by Stanley Appelbaum of Schoenberg's foreword to Pierrot and the poems on which the two works are based.
ISBN 0-486-27885-9
1. String sextets (Violins (2), violas (2), violoncellos (2))—Scores. 2. Monologues with music (Instrumental ensemble)—Scores. I. Dehmel, Richard, 1863–1920. Weib und Welt. II. Schoenberg, Arnold, 1874–1951. Pierrot lunaire. 1994. III. Title: Verklärte Nacht. IV. Title: Pierrot lunaire.
M652.S37 op. 4 1994 93-45854
CIP
M

Manufactured in the United States of America
Dover Publications, Inc., 31 East 2nd Street, Mineola, N.Y. 11501

Contents

GLOSSARY OF GERMAN TERMS

Translations of footnotes and longer score notes appear at the end of this section.

[pp] aber deutlich hörbar, [very soft] but clearly audible
am Griffbrett, on the fingerboard *(sul tasto)*
am Steg, on the bridge *(sul ponticello)*
ärgerlich, angrily
auf der G [D, etc.] Saite, on the G [etc.] string *(sul G)*
ausdrucksv(oll), expressively
äusserst kurz, wie Tropfen, extremely short, like droplets [of sound]

B [also, *in B*], B-flat
Bass-Klarinette [B-Kl.], bass clarinet
bedeutet, means, signifies
begleitend, secondary (accompanying) voice
beiseite, in an undertone *(sotto voce)*
belebend, becoming livelier
beschleunigend, accelerating
bewegt, moving, agitated
[accel.] bis zum Schluss, [accel.] until the end
Bratsche [Br.], viola
breit(er), broad(er)
breiter Auftakt, broad upbeat

col legno gestrichen, struck with the wood of the bow
C-Saite, on the C string *(sul C)*

Dämpfer, mute
Dämpfer aufsetzen, mute on
Dämpfer weg, mute off
deutlich, distinct, clear
doch, yet, but
Doppelgriff es u. h, doublestop E-flat and B
drängend, etwas unruhiger, pressing forward rather nervously
D-Saite, on the D string *(sul D)*
durchaus begleitend, accompanying throughout
durchaus legato, always *legato*

ernst, solemn
erregt, agitated
etwas, somewhat, slightly
etwas belebter, slightly more lively
etwas bewegter, somewhat more animated
etwas gedehnt, somewhat broadly
etwas langsamer, a little slower
etwas rasch(er), somewhat quick(er)
etwas ruhiger, a little more calmly
etwas zögernd, rather hesitant
etwas zurückhalt(end), slightly held back

Flag(eolett), harmonic
Flatterzunge, fluttertongue
fliessend(e), flowing
fliessende, aber abwechslungsreich, flowing, but abundantly modulated
Flöte [Fl. or *gr. Fl.],* flute
flüchtig, fleeting
frei, free

gehende, moving
Geige [G.], violin
gesprochen, spoken
gestossen, driving forward
gestrichen, rushing ahead
gesungen, sung
gezischt, hissed
Griffbrett, fingerboard
Gr(osse) Flöte [gr. Fl.], flute
G-Saite, on the G string *(sul G)*

Hauptstimme, principal voice
hervor(tretend), prominent, to the fore
hüpfend, frisky

immer, always, steadily
immer ganzer Bogen, with a full bow throughout
immer langsamer werdend, becoming continually slower
immer weiter, continually broader
im Takt, in the measure, on the beat
im Zeitmass, in tempo
in abwechslungsreicher Bewegung, with a richly modulated movement
innig, expressive, heartfelt
innig, sehr zart und weich, expressive, very subdued and delicate

kein Pedal, no pedal
kläglich, plaintively
Klang, tone [actual sound of harmonics]
Klarinette [Kl.], clarinet
Klavier [Klav.], piano
Klavier-Auszug, piano reduction [condensed score]
Komisch bedeutsam, with comical self-importance
kurz, short

l.H [linke Hand], left hand
langsam(er), slow(er)
langsamer Walzer, slow waltz
lebhaft bewegt, lively, agitated
lebhafter, livelier
leicht bewegt, freely moving
leise, slight, low [volume]

mässige, moderate
mässig langsam, moderately slow
mässig rasch, moderately quick
mit, with
mit Dämpfer, with the mute on
mit Dämpfung, damped
mit der Rezitation, follow the reciting (speaking) voice
mit schmerzlichem Ausdr(uck), with heartfelt grief
mit Ton gesprochen, spoken with tone (pitch)

Nebenstimme, secondary (accompanying) voice
nimmt, change to [a different instrument]
noch bewegter, still more agitated

ohne, without
ohne Dämpfer, without mute
ohne Pedal, without pedal

plötzlich viel langsamer, suddenly much slower

[quasi] kadenzierend, [in the manner of] a cadenza

r. H. [rechte Hand], right hand
rasch(e), rascher, quick, quicker
rascher werdend, quickening
Rezitation, reciting (speaking) voice
ruhig(er), calm(er)

Schalltrichter hoch, put the bell [of the clarinet] in the air
schneller werdend, becoming faster
schwungvoll, spirited
sehr, very
sehr frei vorzutragen, executed very freely
sehr gross, very big, large
sehr hoch, aber äusserst zart, very high, but extremely delicately
sehr ruhig, ohne Ausdruck, very calm, without expression
sehr ruhig (und gleichmässig), very calm (and even)
sehr voll und gewichtig, very full and heavy
sentimental, sentimental, reflective
später, later
[spicc.] springender Bogen, played *spiccato,* with a bounced bow
steigernd, gradually louder *(crescendo)*
steigernd, beschleunigend, gradually louder and faster *(crescendo e accelerando)*
Stimme(n), voice(s)
stumm niederdrücken, [the piano keys] silently depressed

Takt(e), measure(s), beat(s)
Teil, part, section
ton, tone, sound
tonlos, toneless, unpitched
tonlos geflüstert, unpitched whisper
tonlos niederdrücken, [the piano keys] depressed without sound
trocken, dryly

viel langsamer, much slower
Violoncell(o) [Vcl.], cello
von, from, of, by

warm, warm, ardent
weich, delicate, smooth, tender
weich und lang, smooth and sustained
wieder, again, once more
wieder begleitend, return to an accompanying role
wieder belebter, lively once more
wieder gewöhnlich, return to the usual way of playing *(modo ordinario)*
wieder wie früher, once again as before
wild, rough, fierce, impetuous
wild, leidenschaftlich, turbulent, passionate
wuchtig, weighty, powerful

zart, subdued, gentle
zart doch ausdrucksvoll, gently but expressively
zart hervortreten, gently to the fore
ziemlich bewegte, increasingly agitated
ziemlich rasch, becoming fast
zögernd, hesitant
zurück(treten), receding
zurücktreten, doch innig, receding, but heartfelt

Footnotes and Longer Score Notes

In *Verklärte Nacht:*

Page 4, footnote:
Dieses Zeichen bedeutet ein kleine Luftpause.
This sign [V] denotes a brief pause for breath.

Page 16, footnote:
1. Geige, 2. Bratsche u. 2. Cello spielen ohne Dämpfer; 2. Geige, 1. Bratsche u. 1. Cello mit Dämpfer.
Violin 1, Viola 2 and Cello 2 play without mute; Violin 2, Viola 1 and Cello 1 play with mute.

Page 30, footnote:
Von hier an die nächsten vier Takte sind "am Griffbrett" zu spielen (alle 6 Instrumente), der 5. Takt wieder gewöhnlich.
From here on, the next four measures are to be played on the fingerboard [*sul tasto*] (all 6 instruments), the 5th measure in the ordinary way once more.

Page 32, 3rd bar, tempo marking:
die ♩. *gleich den* ♩ *von früher*
the ♩. equals the previous ♩

Page 34, 6th bar, tempo marking:
die ♩ *langsamer als die frühern* ♪
the ♩ is slower than the previous ♪

In *Pierrot Lunaire:*

"Colombine" / p. 67, footnote [repeated on pp. 70, 81, 95, 98, 101]
┌ ┐ *bedeutet Hauptstimme*
┌ ┐ signifies a principal voice

"Der Dandy" / p. 72, m. 18, voice:
(fast gesungen, mit etwas Ton, sehr gezogen, an die Klarinette anpassend)
(almost sung, with some tone [pitch], very drawn out, following the clarinet line)

"Eine blasse Wäscherin" / p. 74, beginning, top of score:
Die drei Instrumente in vollständig gleicher Klangstärke, alle ohne jeden Ausdruck
The three instruments at completely equal volume, all totally expressionless

[same] / p. 74, beginning, piano (in margin):
(Das Klavier pausiert in diesem Stück)
(The piano does not play in this piece)

[same] / p. 74, beginning, voice:
Die Rezitation soll hier durchaus wie eine Begleitung zu den Instrumenten klingen; sie ist Nebenstimme, Hauptstimme sind die Instrumente.
The speaking voice here should sound throughout like an accompaniment to the instruments; it is a secondary voice, the instruments are the primary voice.

"Valse de Chopin" / p. 77, footnote:
Die mit ┌ *bezeichneten Stellen sind bis zum Zeichen* ┐ *hervorzuheben, espressivo zu spielen, weil sie Haupt- oder I. Nebenstimme sind. Die andern Stimmen haben gegen sie zurückzutreten; sind Begleitung.*
The passages marked ┌ are to be emphasized up to the mark ┐ and played *espressivo* because they are the principal voice or the leading secondary voice. The other voices must recede in their favor; they are the accompaniment.

"Madonna" / p. 82, m. 16, voice:
Sehr ruhig beginnend, nach und nach mächtig steigernd
Beginning very calmly, gradually becoming extremely loud

[same] / p. 82, footnote:
hinaufschleifen, während die angerissene Saite weiterklingt
slide upward, while the sharply plucked string is still vibrating

"Der kranke Mond" / p. 83, m. 25, voice:
(im Ton genau so wie der vorhergehende Takt)
(pitched exactly like the preceding measure)

[same] / p. 83, m. 26, voice:
(dieser Takt anders, aber doch nicht tragisch!!)
(this measure differently, but not tragically!!)

"Nacht" / p. 84, m. 10, voice:
gesungen (womöglich die tieferen Noten)
sung (the lower notes, if possible)

"Gebet an Pierrot" / p. 87, footnote:
Die Rezitation hat die Tonhöhe andeutungsweise zu bringen.
The reciting voice must project the pitch in an indirect way.

"Raub" / p. 89, m. 5, voice:
streng im Takt weiter
continue in strict measure

[same] / p. 91, m. 20, tempo marking:
molto rit. (von ♪ ca 80 bis ♬ ca 100–90)
molto rit. (from ca. ♪ = 80 until ca. ♬ = 100–90)

"Rote Messe" / p. 92, m. 1, piano:
(liegen lassen bis zum Zeichen ✱)
([keep the pedal down] up to the sign ✱)

"Enthauptung" / p. 99, two footnotes:
*) *Hier darf keine Stimme hervortreten; bloss die mit "sf" bezeichneten Stellen haben sich deutlich abzuheben.*
Here, no voice should be prominent; only the passages marked *sf* are to be distinctly emphasized.
+) *bedeutet: pizz. mit der linken Hand*
The sign + indicates a left-hand *pizz.* [cello]

"Heimweh" / p. 108, footnote:
Geige: + + pizz. mit der linken Hand
Violin: + + left-hand *pizz.*

"Parodie" / p. 115, m. 1, clarinet:
Klarinette imitiert genau den Vortrag der Bratsche
The clarinet exactly imitates the viola's phrasing

[same] / p. 118, m. 31, top of score:
Überleitung zu "Mondfleck"
transition to "Mondfleck"

"Serenade" / p. 124, beginning, tempo marking:
Sehr langsamer Walzer (mässige 𝅗𝅥.) ♩ = ca. 120–132; sehr frei vorzutragen
Very slow waltz (moderate 𝅗𝅥.) ♩ = ca. 120–132; executed very freely

VERKLÄRTE NACHT
(Transfigured Night)
OP. 4 (1899)

After Richard Dehmel's poem "Verklärte Nacht"
from *Weib und Welt* (*Woman and World*)

For Two Violins, Two Violas and Two Cellos

VERKLÄRTE NACHT (Transfigured Night)

Poem by Richard Dehmel
from *Weib und Welt (Woman and World)*

English translation by Stanley Appelbaum

<table>
<tr><td>Zwei Menschen gehn durch kahlen, kalten Hain;
der Mond läuft mit, sie schaun hinein.
Der Mond läuft über hohe Eichen,
kein Wölkchen trübt das Himmelslicht,
in das die schwarzen Zacken reichen.
Die Stimme eines Weibes spricht:</td><td>Two people walk through a bare, cold grove;
The moon races along with them, they look into it.
The moon races over tall oaks,
No cloud obscures the light from the sky,
Into which the black points of the boughs reach.
A woman's voice speaks:</td></tr>
<tr><td>Ich trag ein Kind, und nit von Dir,
ich geh in Sünde neben Dir.
Ich hab mich schwer an mir vergangen.
Ich glaubte nicht mehr an ein Glück
und hatte doch ein schwer Verlangen
nach Lebensinhalt, nach Mutterglück</td><td>I'm carrying a child, and not yours,
I walk in sin beside you.
I have committed a great offense against myself.
I no longer believed I could be happy
And yet I had a strong yearning
For something to fill my life, for the joys of motherhood</td></tr>
<tr><td>und Pflicht; da hab ich mich erfrecht,
da liess ich schaudernd mein Geschlecht
von einem fremden Mann umfangen,
und hab mich noch dafür gesegnet.
Nun hat das leben sich gerächt:
nun bin ich Dir, o Dir begegnet.</td><td>And for duty; so I committed an effrontery,
So, shuddering, I allowed my sex
To be embraced by a strange man,
And, on top of that, I blessed myself for it.
Now life has taken its revenge:
Now I have met you, oh, you.</td></tr>
<tr><td>Sie geht mit ungelenkem Schritt.
Sie schaut empor; der Mond läuft mit.
Ihr dunkler Blick ertrinkt in Licht.
Die Stimme eines Mannes spricht:</td><td>She walks with a clumsy gait,
She looks up; the moon is racing along.
Her dark gaze is drowned in light.
A man's voice speaks:</td></tr>
<tr><td>Das Kind, das Du empfangen hast,
sei Deiner Seele keine Last,
o sieh, wie klar das Weltall schimmert!
Es ist ein Glanz um Alles her,
Du treibst mit mir auf kaltem Meer,
doch eine eigne Wärme flimmert
von Dir in mich, von mir in Dich.
Die wird das fremde Kind verklären,
Du wirst es mir, von mir gebären;
Du hast den Glanz in mich gebracht,
Du hast mich selbst zum Kind gemacht.</td><td>May the child you conceived
Be no burden to your soul;
Just see how brightly the universe is gleaming!
There's a glow around everything;
You are floating with me on a cold ocean,
But a special warmth flickers
From you into me, from me into you.
It will transfigure the strange man's child.
You will bear the child for me, as if it were mine;
You have brought the glow into me,
You have made me like a child myself.</td></tr>
<tr><td>Er fasst sie um die starken Hüften.
Ihr Atem küsst sich in den Lüften.
Zwei Menschen gehn durch hohe, helle Nacht.</td><td>He grasps her around her ample hips.
Their breath kisses in the breeze.
Two people walk through the lofty, bright night.</td></tr>
</table>

Sehr langsam.
1. Geige.
2. Geige.
1. Bratsche.
2. Bratsche.
1. Violoncello.
2. Violoncello.
immer leise
pp
immer leise
pp
immer leise
pp
immer leise
pp
immer leise
pp
immer leise
pp
immer leise
immer leise
immer leise
immer leise

*) Dieses Zeichen bedeutet eine kleine Luftpause.

rit.
steigernd cresc.
accel.
cresc.
molto rit.
Etwas bewegter.
steigernd
cresc.

C
rit.
tempo
dim.
p dim.
p
sf
ff
f

pizz.
f
pizz.
f
rit.
mit Dämpfer
arco
ausdrucksv.
pp
mit Dampfer
arco
pp
ausdrucksv.
mit Dämpfer
sf
arco
p
mit Dämpfer
pizz.
arco
mit Dämpfer
P mit schmerzlichem Ausdr.
mit Dämpfer
pizz.
pp
D
mp

rit.
E
ohne Dämpfer
ohne Dämpfer
G Saite
ohne Dämpfer
ohne Dämpfer
ohne Dämpfer
ohne Dämpfer
G Saite
steigernd
cresc. e accel.
steigernd
cresc. e accel.
steigernd
cresc. e accel.
steigernd
cresc. e accel.
steigernd
cresc. e accel.
steigernd
cresc. e accel.

Lebhafter.
ff
ff
ff
ff
3
ff
sf
ff
5
3
3
3
5
3
rit.
rit.
5
rit.
rit.
rit.
5
5

Etwas belebter.
Etwas zurückhaltend.
warm
warm
dim.
Wieder belebter.

Etwas zurückhaltend.
warm
pp
warm
pp
pp
pp
pp
pp
dim. e rit.
Lebhafter.
p
p
p
p
p
p
p
p
p
p
mf
mf
mf
mf
mf
f
f
f
f
f
f
f

Breiter.
p dolce
p dolce
p dolce
p dolce
p dolce

Etwas ruhiger.
pp
pp
pp
pp
pp
pp
rit.
p
dolce
p
dolce
p
dolce
p
warm
warm
warm
warm
cresc.
hervor-
marc.
mf
rit.
F
tretend
p
p
p
p

warm
warm
warm
warm
mf
mf
Drängend,
etwas unruhiger.

steigernd
cresc. e accel.
rascher werdend
steigernd, molto cresc. e accel.
Lebhaft bewegt.

*) 1. Geige, 2. Bratsche u. 2. Cello spielen ohne Dämpfer; 2. Geige, 1. Bratsche u. 1. Cello mit Dämpfer.

accel.
arco
pizz.
(trem.)
wild
G

pizz.
rit.
accel.
accel.
arco
rit.
pizz.

Noch bewegter.
f
arco
p
pizz.
ff
cresc.

H
pp
ppp
p
pp
arco
f
ohne Dämpfer.
steigernd
ff

Rascher.
ohne Dämpfer.
ohne Dämpfer.
molto cresc.
molto cresc.
molto cresc.
molto cresc.
molto cresc.
molto cresc.

Schneller werdend.
J
Sehr breit.
molto rit.
Sehr langsam.
G Saite
dim.

dim. e rit.
K
G Saite
sehr ausdrucksvoll
espress.
p dim.
G Saite
Schwer betont.
G Saite
G Saite

L
etwas zurückhalt.
sehr zart
pp
sff
C Saite
ff
sf

rit.
pp
p
pppp

Sehr breit und langsam.
weich
weich
p zart
p zart doch
espress.
ausdrucksvoll
M
innig
cresc.
espress.
innig
cresc.
cresc.
cresc.
cresc.

rit.
rit.
mit Dämpfer.
mit Dämpfer.
mit Dämpfer.
mit Dämpfer.
Flag.
Flag.
mit Dämpfer.
Flag.
mit Dämpfer.
Flag.

pp
pp
pizz.
pp
Flag.
weich und lang
pizz.
weich und lang
pizz.
N
innig, sehr zart und weich.
p
pp
pp
pp arco
arco

ausdrucksvoll
cresc.
p
cresc.
ausdrucksvoll
p
cresc.
p
p
p

*) Von hier an die nächsten vier Takte sind „am Griffbrett" zu spielen (alle 6 Instrumente) der 5. Takt wieder gewöhnlich.

Wieder wie früher.
rit.
wieder gewöhnlich
ppp
pp
p
espress.
poco
cresc.
poco cresc.
cresc.

cresc.
cresc.
cresc.
rit.
f
ff
die ♩. gleich den ♩ von früher.
rit.
sehr innig und warm
mf
p
Im Zeitmass.
G saite
zurücktr.
ppp
ausdrucksvoll doch
zart hervortreten
mp

espress.
O
D Saite
G Saite
pp
ten.
ppp
pp
mf
ten.
espr.
mf
f

steigernd, beschleunigend
p cresc.
p cresc.
p cresc.
p cresc.
p cresc.
p cresc.
die ♩ langsamer als die frühern ♪
f
fp
f
p
f
f
p
f
p
ausdrucksvoll
f

ohne Dämpfer
sehr warm
rit.
ohne Dämpfer
sehr warm
p sehr weich
p
sf
p sehr weich
sfp
p
P a tempo
f
fp
f
fp
f
ohne Dämpfer
p
p
p
ohne Dämpfer
p
ohne Dämpfer
p
ohne Dämpfer

poco a poco cresc.
steigernd
poco a poco cresc.
steigernd
poco a poco cresc.
steigernd
poco a poco cresc.
steigernd
poco a poco cresc.
steigernd
ohne Dämpfer
poco a poco cresc.
steigernd
cresc.
cresc.
cresc.
cresc.
cresc.
cresc.
cresc.
cresc.
cresc.
cresc.
cresc.
cresc.

Etwas bewegter.

Q
ff
rit.

R Etwas bewegt.
pp zart
pp zart
p
p
p
dolce
pp
pp
p
p
p
p
steigernd
mf
steigernd
steigernd
steigernd
steigernd
steigernd

steigernd
S
beschleunigend
cresc.
cresc.
cresc.
cresc.
cresc.
cresc.

molto rit.

gross
ff espress.
pp sehr zart
pp
pp
ausdrucksvoll
mp
espress.
mf
sfp
espress.

T
p
p
cresc.
mf
cresc.
f
cresc.
ff
fp

rit.
D Saite
dim.
G Saite
p espr.
fp
poco rit.
G Saite
rit.
molto rit.
mit Dämpfer
p dolce
U Sehr ruhig.
pp zurücktreten, doch innig
mf espress.

espr.
hervort.
zart
p
pp
pp weich
ppp
zurückt.
pp
p
mf espr.
fp
p espr.
fp weich
ppp zurückt.

V
espr.
p
espr.
p
p
6
p
p espr.
p
6
schrzart
p
p
p
mf
f

steigernd
cresc.
molto rit.
pp
f
ff

molto rit.
Sehr gross.
ff
sf
dim.
sfp
pp dolciss.
G Saite
pp
rit.
W
D Saite
zart

rit.
zart
pp
dim.
zart
dim.
pp
dim.
dim.
pp
dim.
dim.
X
pp
pp
pizz.
pp
pp
pizz.
pp
pizz.
pp

Klang
Flag.
pp
ppp
Klang
Flag.
pp
ppp
Klang
Flag.
D Saite
pp
ppp
Klang
Flag.
pp
ppp
Flag.
Klang
pp
ppp
Flag.
Klang
pp
ppp
pppp
pppp
pppp

PIERROT LUNAIRE
OP. 21 (1912)

Three Times Seven Poems by Albert Giraud
German Translation from the French by Otto Erich Hartleben

For Speaking Voice, Piano, Flute (+ Piccolo),
Clarinet (+ Bass Clarinet), Violin (+ Viola) and Cello

Composer's Foreword

The melody given in notation in the vocal part (with a few specially indicated exceptions) is *not* intended to be sung. The performer has the task of transforming it into a *speech melody* [*Sprechmelodie*], taking the prescribed pitches well into account. He accomplishes this by:

I. adhering to the rhythm as precisely as if he were singing; that is, with no more freedom than he would allow himself if it were a sung melody;

II. being precisely aware of the difference between a *sung tone* and a *spoken tone:* the sung tone maintains the pitch unaltered; the spoken tone does indicate it, but immediately abandons it again by falling or rising. But the performer must take great care not to lapse into a singsong speech pattern. That is absolutely not intended. The goal is certainly not at all a realistic, natural speech. On the contrary, the difference between ordinary speech and speech that collaborates in a musical form must be made plain. But it should not call singing to mind, either.

Furthermore, the following should be said about the performance:

The performers' task here is at no time to derive the mood and character of the individual pieces from the meaning of the words, but always solely from the music. To the extent that the tonepainterly representation [*tonmalerische Darstellung*] of the events and feelings in the text were of importance to the composer, it will be found in the music anyway. Wherever the performer fails to find it, he must resist adding something that the composer did not intend. If he did so, he would not be adding, but subtracting.

ARNOLD SCHOENBERG

[English translation by Stanley Appelbaum]

Contents and Instrumentation

[*Note:* The speaking voice (*Rezitation*) performs throughout the twenty-one pieces in this work. The instrumental ensemble varies from one piece to the next, drawing upon five performers playing eight instruments: flute (doubles piccolo), clarinet in A (in B♭ in No. 18) (doubles B♭ bass clarinet), violin (doubles viola), cello and piano. The instrumentation below each title follows the wording style in the original score.]

I. Teil (Part I)

II. Teil (Part II)

III. Teil (Part III)

Nach dem I. und II. Teil lange Pausen. Innerhalb der Teile sind einzelne Stücke, wie angegeben, durch Pausen deutlich zu trennen, während andere, durch Zwischenspiele verbunden, unmittelbar ins folgende übergehen.

After Parts I and II, long pauses. Within the parts, some of the individual pieces, as indicated, are to be clearly separated by pauses, whereas others, connected by transitional music, segue at once to the following number.

PIERROT LUNAIRE

Three Times Seven Poems by Albert Giraud
German Translation from the French by Otto Erich Hartleben

English Translation by Stanley Appelbaum

I. TEIL (Part I)

1. MONDESTRUNKEN (DRUNK WITH MOONLIGHT)

Den Wein, den man mit Augen trinkt,
Giesst Nachts der Mond in Wogen nieder,
Und eine Springflut überschwemmt
Den stillen Horizont.

Gelüste, schauerlich und süss,
Durchschwimmen ohne Zahl die Fluten!
Den Wein, den man mit Augen trinkt,
Giesst Nachts der Mond in Wogen nieder.

Der Dichter, den die Andacht treibt,
Berauscht sich an dem heilgen Tranke,
Gen Himmel wendet er verzückt
Das Haupt und taumelnd saugt und schlürft er
Den Wein, den man mit Augen trinkt.

The wine that one drinks with one's eyes
Is poured down in waves by the moon at night,
And a spring tide overflows
The silent horizon.

Lusts, thrilling and sweet,
Float numberless through the waters!
The wine that one drinks with one's eyes
Is poured down in waves by the moon at night.

The poet, urged on by his devotions,
Becomes intoxicated with the sacred beverage;
Enraptured, he turns toward heaven
His head, and, staggering, sucks and sips
The wine that one drinks with one's eyes.

2. COLOMBINE (COLUMBINE)

Des Mondlichts bleiche Blüten,
Die weissen Wunderrosen,
Blühn in den Julinächten—
O bräch ich eine nur!

Mein banges Leid zu lindern,
Such ich am dunklen Strome
Des Mondlichts bleiche Blüten,
Die weissen Wunderrosen.

Gestillt wär all mein Sehnen,
Dürft ich so märchenheimlich,
So selig leis—entblättern
Auf deine braunen Haare
Des Mondlichts bleiche Blüten!

The moonlight's pale blossoms,
The white wonder-roses,
Bloom in the July nights—
Oh, if I could just pick one!

To alleviate my anxious sorrow,
I seek along the dark stream
The moonlight's pale blossoms,
The white wonder-roses.

All my yearning would be stilled
If I were permitted—as secretly as in a fairy tale,
So blissfully softly—to scatter
Onto your brown hair the petals of
The moonlight's pale blossoms!

3. DER DANDY (THE DANDY)

Mit einem phantastischen Lichtstrahl
Erleuchtet der Mond die krystallnen Flakons
Auf dem schwarzen, hochheiligen Waschtisch
Des schweigenden Dandys von Bergamo.

In tönender, bronzener Schale
Lacht hell die Fontäne, metallischen Klangs.
Mit einem phantastischen Lichtstrahl
Erleuchtet der Mond die krystallnen Flakons.

Pierrot mit wächsernem Antlitz
Steht sinnend und denkt: wie er heute sich schminkt?
Fort schiebt er das Rot und des Orients Grün
Und bemalt sein Gesicht in erhabenem Stil
Mit einem phantastischen Mondstrahl.

With a fantastic ray of light
The moon illuminates the crystal flacons
On the black, sacrosanct washstand
Of the silent dandy from Bergamo.

In the resounding bronze basin
The water jet laughs brightly, with a metallic sound.
With a fantastic ray of light
The moon illuminates the crystal flacons.

Pierrot with his waxen face
Stands meditatively and thinks: how shall he make up today?
He shoves aside the red, and the green of the Orient,
And paints his face in a noble style
With a fantastic moonbeam.

4. EINE BLASSE WÄSCHERIN (A PALLID WASHERWOMAN)

Eine blasse Wäscherin
Wäscht zur Nachtzeit bleiche Tücher;
Nackte, silberweisse Arme
Streckt sie nieder in die Flut.

Durch die Lichtung schleichen Winde,
Leis bewegen sie den Strom.
Eine blasse Wäscherin
Wäscht zur Nachtzeit bleiche Tücher.

Und die sanfte Magd des Himmels,
Von den Zweigen zart umschmeichelt,
Breitet auf die dunklen Wiesen
Ihre lichtgewobnen Linnen—
Eine blasse Wäscherin.

A pallid washerwoman
Washes pale cloths in the nighttime,
She stretches bare, silvery white arms
Down into the flowing water.

Winds steal through the clearing,
Gently they ruffle the stream.
A pallid washerwoman
Washes pale cloths in the nighttime.

And the gentle maid of heaven,
Daintily flattered by the boughs,
Spreads out on the dark meadows
Her linens woven of light—
A pallid washerwoman.

5. VALSE DE CHOPIN

Wie ein blasser Tropfen Bluts
Färbt die Lippen einer Kranken,
Also ruht auf diesen Tönen
Ein vernichtungssüchtger Reiz.

Wilder Lust Akkorde stören
Der Verzweiflung eisgen Traum—
Wie ein blasser Tropfen Bluts
Färbt die Lippen einer Kranken.

Heiss und jauchzend, süss und schmachtend,
Melancholisch düstrer Walzer,
Kommst mir nimmer aus den Sinnen!
Haftest mir an den Gedanken,
Wie ein blasser Tropfen Bluts!

As a pale drop of blood
colors a sick woman's lips,
Thus there rests upon these notes
A charm that hungers for annihilation.

Chords of wild pleasure disturb
The icy dream of desperation—
As a pale drop of blood
Colors a sick woman's lips.

Hot and exultant, sweet and languishing,
Melancholy, somber waltz,
I can't get you out of my head!
You adhere to my thoughts
Like a pale drop of blood!

6. MADONNA

Steig, o Mutter aller Schmerzen,
Auf den Altar meiner Verse!
Blut aus deinen magern Brüsten
Hat des Schwertes Wut vergossen.

Deine ewig frischen Wunden
Gleichen Augen, rot und offen.
Steig, o Mutter aller Schmerzen,
Auf den Altar meiner Verse!

In den abgezehrten Händen
Hältst du deines Sohnes Leiche,
Ihn zu zeigen aller Menschheit—
Doch der Blick der Menschen meidet
Dich, o Mutter aller Schmerzen!

Step, O Mother of all sorrows,
Onto the altar of my verses!
Blood from your thin breasts
Has been shed by the fury of the sword.

Your eternally fresh wounds
Resemble eyes, red and open.
Step, O Mother of all sorrows,
Onto the altar of my verses!

In your emaciated hands
You hold your son's corpse,
To show him to all mankind—
But the gaze of men avoids
You, O Mother of all sorrows!

7. DER KRANKE MOND (THE SICK MOON)

Du nächtig todeskranker Mond
Dort auf des Himmels schwarzem Pfühl,
Dein Blick, so fiebernd übergross,
Bannt mich, wie fremde Melodie.

An unstillbarem Liebesleid
Stirbst du, an Sehnsucht, tief erstickt,
Du nächtig todeskranker Mond,
Dort auf des Himmels schwarzem Pfühl.

Den Liebsten, der im Sinnenrausch
Gedankenlos zur Liebsten geht,
Belustigt deiner Strahlen Spiel—
Dein bleiches, qualgebornes Blut,
Du nächtig todeskranker Mond!

You moon, gloomy and sick to death
There on the black cushion of the sky,
Your eye, so feverishly enlarged,
Casts a spell over me like a strange melody.

You are dying of an inconsolable sorrow of love,
Dying of longing, totally suffocated,
You moon, gloomy and sick to death
There on the black cushion of the sky.

The lover, who in ecstasy
Is going off, carefree, to his sweetheart,
Is amused by the play of your beams—
Your pale, torment-born blood,
You moon, gloomy and sick to death!

II. TEIL (Part II)

8. NACHT (NIGHT)
(Passacaglia)

Finstre, schwarze Riesenfalter
Töteten der Sonne Glanz.
Ein geschlossnes Zauberbuch,
Ruht der Horizont—verschwiegen.

Aus dem Qualm verlorner Tiefen
Steigt ein Duft, Erinnrung mordend!
Finstre, schwarze Riesenfalter
Töteten der Sonne Glanz.

Und vom Himmel erdenwärts
Senken sich mit schweren Schwingen
Unsichtbar die Ungetüme
Auf die Menschenherzen nieder . . .
Finstre, schwarze Riesenfalter.

Dark, black giant moths
Killed the brightness of the sun.
Like a closed book of magic spells,
The horizon rests—mutely.

Out of the vapor of lost depths
Arises a fragrance, murdering all memory!
Dark, black giant moths
Killed the brightness of the sun.

And from the sky earthwards
There descend on heavy pinions,
Invisible, the monsters
Onto human hearts . . .
Dark, black giant moths.

9. GEBET AN PIERROT (PRAYER TO PIERROT)

Pierrot! Mein Lachen
Hab ich verlernt!
Das Bild des Glanzes
Zerfloss—zerfloss!

Schwarz weht die Flagge
Mir nun vom Mast.
Pierrot! Mein Lachen
Hab ich verlernt!

O gib mir wieder,
Rossarzt der Seele,
Schneemann der Lyrik,
Durchlaucht vom Monde,
Pierrot—mein Lachen!

Pierrot! My laughter—
I've forgotten how to laugh!
The image of brightness
Dissolved—dissolved!

A black flag waves
On my mast now.
Pierrot! My laughter—
I've forgotten how to laugh!

Oh, give me back—
Horse doctor of the soul,
Snowman of lyricism,
Your Grace of the moon,
Pierrot—my laughter!

10. RAUB (THEFT)

Rote, fürstliche Rubine,
Blutge Tropfen alten Ruhmes,
Schlummern in den Totenschreinen,
Drunten in den Grabgewölben.

Nachts, mit seinen Zechkumpanen,
Steigt Pierrot hinab—zu rauben
Rote, fürstliche Rubine,
Blutge Tropfen alten Ruhmes.

Doch da—sträuben sich die Haare,
Bleiche Furcht bannt sie am Platze:
Durch die Finsternis—wie Augen!—
Stieren aus den Totenschreinen
Rote, fürstliche Rubine.

Red, princely rubies,
Bloody drops of antique glory,
Slumber in the coffins,
Down in the burial vaults.

At night, with his drinking companions,
Pierrot descends—to steal
Red, princely rubies,
Bloody drops of antique glory.

But there—their hair stands on end,
Pale fear nails them to the spot:
Through the darkness —like eyes!—
There stare from the coffins
Red, princely rubies.

11. ROTE MESSE (RED MASS)

Zu grausem Abendmahle,
Beim Blendeglanz des Goldes,
Beim Flackerschein der Kerzen,
Naht dem Altar—Pierrot!

For a hideous Communion,
In the dazzling shine of gold,
In the wavering light of tapers,
Pierrot approaches the altar!

Die Hand, die gottgeweihte,
Zerreisst die Priesterkleider
Zu grausem Abendmahle,
Beim Blendglanz des Goldes.

Mit segnender Geberde
Zeigt er den bangen Seelen
Die triefend rote Hostie:
Sein Herz—in blutgen Fingern—
Zu grausem Abendmahle!

His hand, consecrated to God,
Rips the priestly garments
For a hideous Communion
In the dazzling shine of gold.

With a gesture of benediction
He shows to the frightened souls
The dripping red Host:
His heart—in bloody fingers—
For a hideous Communion!

12. GALGENLIED (GALLOWS SONG)

Die dürre Dirne
Mit langem Halse
Wird seine letzte
Geliebte sein.

In seinem Hirne
Steckt wie ein Nagel
Die dürre Dirne
Mit langem Halse.

Schlank wie die Pinie,
Am Hals ein Zöpfchen—
Wollüstig wird sie
Den Schelm umhalsen,
Die dürre Dirne!

The scraggy harlot
With a long neck
Will be his last
Lover.

In his brain
Is stuck like a nail
The scraggy harlot
With a long neck.

Slender as a pine,
On her neck a little braid—
Lustfully she will
Hug the rogue's neck,
The scraggy harlot!

13. ENTHAUPTUNG (BEHEADING)

Der Mond, ein blankes Türkenschwert
Auf einem schwarzen Seidenkissen,
Gespenstisch gross—dräut er hinab
Durch schmerzensdunkle Nacht.

Pierrot irrt ohne Rast umher
Und starrt empor in Todesängsten
Zum Mond, dem blanken Türkenschwert
Auf einem schwarzen Seidenkissen.

Es schlottern unter ihm die Knie,
Ohnmächtig bricht er jäh zusammen.
Er wähnt: es sause strafend schon
Auf seinen Sündenhals hernieder
Der Mond, das blanke Türkenschwert.

The moon, a gleaming scimitar
On a black silk pillow,
Spectrally large—sends down threats
Through the sorrow-dark night.

Pierrot wanders about restlessly
And stares up in mortal anguish
At the moon, the gleaming scimitar
On a black silk pillow.

His knees shake under him,
All at once he falls into a faint.
He imagines that in punishment there already whizzes
Down onto his sinful neck
The moon, the gleaming scimitar.

14. DIE KREUZE (THE CROSSES)

Heilge Kreuze sind die Verse,
Dran die Dichter stumm verbluten,
Blindgeschlagen von der Geier
Flatterndem Gespensterschwarme!

In den Leibern schwelgten Schwerter,
Prunkend in des Blutes Scharlach!
Heilge Kreuze sind die Verse,
Dran die Dichter stumm verbluten.

Tot das Haupt—erstarrt die Locken—
Fern, verweht der Lärm des Pöbels.
Langsam sinkt die Sonne nieder,
Eine rote Königskrone.—
Heilge Kreuze sind die Verse!

Verses are holy crosses
On which poets silently bleed to death,
Stricken blind by the fluttering
Ghostly swarm of vultures!

In their bodies swords have reveled,
Gaudy in the blood's scarlet!
Verses are holy crosses
On which poets silently bleed to death.

Dead the head—stiff the tresses—
Far, drifted away, the noise of the commoners.
Slowly the sun sets,
A red royal crown.—
Verses are holy crosses!

III. TEIL (Part III)

15. HEIMWEH (HOMESICKNESS)

Lieblich klagend—ein krystallnes Seufzen
Aus Italiens alter Pantomime,
Klingts herüber: wie Pierrot so hölzern,
So modern sentimental geworden.

Und es tönt durch seines Herzens Wüste,
Tönt gedämpft durch alle Sinne wieder,
Lieblich klagend—ein krystallnes Seufzen
Aus Italiens alter Pantomime.

Da vergisst Pierrot die Trauermienen!
Durch den bleichen Feuerschein des Mondes,
Durch des Lichtmeers Fluten—schweift die Sehnsucht
Kühn hinauf, empor zum Heimathimmel,
Lieblich klagend—ein krystallnes Seufzen!

Sweetly lamenting—a crystalline sigh
From Italy's antique pantomime—
The sound comes to us: that Pierrot has become
So wooden, so fashionably sentimental.

And it sounds through his heart's wilderness,
Reechoes, muffled, through all his senses,
Sweetly lamenting—a crystalline sigh
From Italy's old pantomime.

Then Pierrot forgets his sad expressions!
Through the pale firelight of the moon,
Through the waves of the sea of light—longing strays
Boldly upward, up to its native sky,
Sweetly lamenting—a crystalline sigh!

16. GEMEINHEIT (FOUL PLAY)

In den blanken Kopf Cassanders,
Dessen Schrein die Luft durchzetert,
Bohrt Pierrot mit Heuchlermienen,
Zärtlich—einen Schädelbohrer!

Darauf stopft er mit dem Daumen
Seinen echten türkschen Tabak
In den blanken Kopf Cassanders,
Dessen Schrein die Luft durchzetert!

Dann dreht er ein Rohr von Weichsel
Hinten in die glatte Glatze
Und behaglich schmaucht und pafft er
Seinen echten türkschen Tabak
Aus dem blanken Kopf Cassanders!

Into the shiny head of Cassander,
Whose cries pierce the air,
Pierrot, with hypocritical looks,
Tenderly inserts—a trephine!

Then with his thumb he stuffs
His genuine Turkish tobacco
Into the shiny head of Cassander,
Whose cries pierce the air!

Then he twists a cherry-wood tube
Into the back of the smooth bald head,
And he comfortably smokes and puffs
His genuine Turkish tobacco
Out of the shiny head of Cassander!

17. PARODIE (PARODY)

Stricknadeln, blank and blinkend,
In ihrem grauen Haar,
Sitzt die Duenna murmelnd,
Im roten Röckchen da.

Sie wartet in der Laube,
Sie liebt Pierrot mit Schmerzen,
Stricknadeln, blank und blinkerd,
In ihrem grauen Haar.

Da plötzlich—horch!—ein Wispern!
Ein Windhauch kichert leise:
Der mond, der böse Spötter,
Äfft nach mit seinen Strahlen—
Stricknadeln, blink und blank.

Knitting needles, shiny and gleaming,
In her gray hair,
The duenna sits mumbling
There in her red skirt.

She waits in the grove,
She loves Pierrot painfully,
Knitting needles, shiny and gleaming,
In her gray hair.

Then suddenly—listen!—a whispering!
A wind current giggles softly:
The moon, the spiteful mocker,
Imitates with its beams—
Knitting needles, gleam and shine.

18. DER MONDFLECK (THE MOON SPOT)

Einen weissen Fleck des hellen Mondes
Auf dem Rücken seines schwarzen Rockes,
So spaziert Pierrot im lauen Abend,
Aufzusuchen Glück und Abenteuer.

A white spot of the bright moonlight
On the back of his black coat,
Thus Pierrot strolls on the warm evening,
Looking for good fortune and adventures.

Plötzlich stört ihn was an seinem Anzug,
Er besieht sich rings und findet richtig—
Einen weissen Fleck des hellen Mondes
Auf dem Rücken seines schwarzen Rockes.

Warte! denkt er: das ist so ein Gipsfleck!
Wischt und wischt, doch—bringt ihn nicht herunter!
Und so geht er, giftgeschwollen, weiter,
Reibt und reibt bis an den frühen Morgen—
Einen weissen Fleck des hellen Mondes.

Suddenly something on his clothing bothers him;
He looks himself all over and finds it precisely—
A white spot of the bright moonlight
On the back of his black coat.

"Wait!" he thinks: "It's some plaster spot!"
He wipes and wipes it but—can't wipe it away!
And so he walks onward, swollen with venom,
Rubs and rubs until early in the morning—
A white spot of the bright moonlight.

19. SERENADE

Mit groteskem Riesenbogen
Kratzt Pierrot auf seiner Bratsche,
Wie der Storch auf einem Beine,
Knipst er trüb ein Pizzicato.

Plötzlich naht Cassander—wütend
Ob des nächtigen Virtuosen—
Mit groteskem Riesenbogen
Kratzt Pierrot auf seiner Bratsche.

Von sich wirft er jetzt die Bratsche:
Mit der delikaten Linken
Fasst er den Kahlkopf am Kragen—
Träumend spielt er auf der Glatze
Mit groteskem Riesenbogen.

With a grotesque gigantic bow
Pierrot scrapes on his viola,
Like the stork on one leg,
He mournfully plucks a pizzicato.

Suddenly Cassander approaches—furious
Over the nocturnal virtuoso—
With a grotesque gigantic bow
Pierrot scrapes on his viola.

Now he throws aside the viola:
With his delicate left hand
He seizes the bald man by the collar—
Dreamily he plays on the bald head
With a grotesque gigantic bow.

20. HEIMFAHRT (JOURNEY HOME)
(Barcarole)

Der Mondstrahl ist das Ruder,
Seerose dient als Boot:
Drauf fährt Pierrot gen Süden
Mit gutem Reisewind.

Der Strom summt tiefe Skalen
Und wiegt den leichten Kahn.
Der Mondstrahl ist das Ruder,
Seerose dient als Boot.

Nach Bergamo, zur Heimat,
Kehrt nun Pierrot zurück,
Schwach dämmert schon im Osten
Der grüne Horizont.
—Der Mondstrahl ist das Ruder.

The moonbeam is the oar,
The water lily serves as the boat:
On it Pierrot travels south
Wafted by a favorable wind.

The river hums low scales
And rocks the light craft.
The moonbeam is the oar,
The water lily serves as the boat.

To Bergamo, his homeland,
Pierrot now returns;
In the east the green horizon
Is already visible in the pale daybreak.
—The moonbeam is the oar.

21. O ALTER DUFT (O ANCIENT FRAGRANCE)

O alter Duft aus Märchenzeit,
Berauschest wieder meine Sinne!
Ein närrisch Heer von Schelmerein
Durchschwirrt die leichte Luft.

Ein glückhaft Wünschen macht mich froh
Nach Freuden, die ich lang verachtet:
O alter Duft aus Märchenzeit,
Berauschest wieder mich!

All meinen Unmut geb ich preis;
Aus meinem sonnumrahmten Fenster
Beschau ich frei die liebe Welt
Und träum hinaus in selge Weiten . . .
O alter Duft—aus Märchenzeit!

O ancient fragrance from the age of fairy tales,
Again you intoxicate my senses!
A foolish host of merry pranks
Flits through the gentle breeze.

A happy desire for joys
That I long contemned makes me cheerful:
O ancient fragrance from the age of fairy tales,
Again you intoxicate me!

I give up all my ill humor;
Through my sunshine-framed window
I freely observe the dear world
And my dreams travel into blissful distances . . .
O ancient fragrance—from the age of fairy tales!

I. Teil.

1. Mondestrunken.

poco rit.
Tempo
Fl.
G.
pp
auf der D-Saite
G-Saite
p dolce espress.
15
(kein Pedal!)
sf
D-Saite
hervor
Ge - lü - ste, schau - er - lich und
20
süß —, durch - schwimmen oh - ne Zahl die Flu - - - ten!
legato
fp

Fl.
G.
am Steg
pizz.
pp
DenWein, denman mit Au - gen trinkt, gießt nachts derMond in Wo - gen
stacc.
25
nie - - dor.
rit.
immer pizz.
Der
Tempo
Vcl.
f molto espress.
30
Dich - ter, dendie An - - dachttreibt, be - rauscht sich an dem heil - gen
f espress.

Fl.
G.
Vcl.
molto rit.
arco
Tran - ke, gen Him - mel wen-det er ver-zückt das Haupt
Tempo
pp subito
ppp
glissando
35 Tempo
und tau - melnd saugt und schlürft er den Wein, den man mit Au - gen
molto legato
poco rit.
pizz.
spiccato
39 molto rit.
trinkt.
folgt: Colombine.
ausgiebige Pause (quasi im Takt)
(Klav., Geige, später dazu Fl., Klar.)
Segue to "Colombine"
after a significant pause
(almost in tempo)

2. Colombine.

┌ ┐ bedeutet Hauptstimme.

rall.
pesante
ruhig
Mein banges Leid zu lin-dern, such ich am dunklen
etwas ruhiger
espr.
dolce
cresc.
Stro - me des Mond - lichts blei - che Blü - ten, die wei - ßen
poco cresc.
Wun - der - ro - sen.
senza Ped.
rit.
Ge -
stillt wär all mein Seh-nen, dürft ich so mär-chen - heim - lich,
so

A significant pause, then go on to **"Der Dandy"**

3. Der Dandy.

⌈ ⌉ bedeutet Hauptstimme.

etwas langsamer
Pic.
Kl. (A)
espress.
rit.
(gesungen)
(gesprochen)
(tonlos geflüstert)
(mit Ton gesprochen)
schwar - zen, hoch - - hei - li - gen Wasch - tisch des
langsam
schwei-genden Dan - dys von Ber - ga - mo. In tö - nender,
Tempo
bron - ze - ner Scha - le lacht hell die Fon - tä - ne, me - tal - lischen Klangs.
l. H.

Flatterzunge
Pic.
Kl. (A)
ppp
sf
p
15
(gesungen)
pp
(tonlos)
(gesungen) (gesprochen)
Mit ei - nem phan - ta - sti - schen Licht - strahl
rit.
molto rit.
pp subito
(fast gesungen, mit etwas Ton, sehr gezogen, an die Klarinette anpassend)
20 molto rit.
erleuch - tet der Mond die krystall - nen Fla - kons.
pp stacc.
dim.
langsamer
f
Pi - er - rot mit wäch - sernem Ant - litz steht sinnend und denkt: —
sf
pp

Pic.
Kl. (A)
wie er heu - te sich schminkt?
Fort schiebt er das
l. H.
r. H.
accel.
Rot und des O - ri - ents Grün und bemalt sein Gesicht in er - ha - be - nem Stil
non legato
tonlos niederdrücken
(Flag.)
ohne Pedal
immer ohne Pedal
rasch
nimmt gr. Fl.
(tonlos geflüstert)
mit einem phanta - stischen Mond - strahl.
möglichst kürze Pause; folgt:
Eine blasse Wäscherin.
Flöte, Klarinette (A)
Geige (mit Dämpfer)
After the briefest possible pause, go on to
"Eine blasse Wäscherin"

4. Eine blasse Wäscherin.

Fl.
Kl. (A)
G.
Tü - cher; nack - te, sil - ber - wei - ße Ar - me streckt sie nie - der in die
3
immer ppp
pizz.
arco
sf
am Steg
10
Flut. Durch die Lichtung schleichen Win - de, leis be - we - gen sie den Strom.
tr
6
col legno gestrichen
(sehr ruhig)
Ei - ne blas - se Wä - sche - rin wäscht zur Nachtzeit blei - che

Fl.
Kl. (A)
G.
arco
G-Saite
Flag.
(gesungen)
pp
Tü-cher. Und die sanf-te Magd des Himmels, von den Zweigen zart umschmeichelt, brei-tet
15
(gesprochen)
auf die dunk-len Wie-sen ih-re licht-ge-wo-be-nen Lin-nen—
sf
ei-ne blas-se Wä-scherin.
ohne jede Pause, gleich anschließend:
Valse de Chopin.
(Klavier, Flöte, Klarinette.)
Without any pause, segue directly into "Valse de Chopin"

5. Valse de Chopin.

Die mit ┌ bezeichneten Stellen sind bis zum Zeichen ┐ hervorzuheben, espressivo zu spielen, weil sie Haupt- oder I. Nebenstimme sind. Die andern Stimmen haben gegen sie zurückzutreten; sind Begleitung.

Fl.
Kl. (A)
Tö_nen ein ver_nich_tungs_sücht'_ _ger Reiz.
stacc.
weich
espr.
schwungvoll
durchaus legato
p dolce espress.
p dolce
f
Wil_ _der Lust___ Ak_kor_ _de stö_ _ren der Verzweiflung
poco rit.
a tempo
p dim.
pp
eis_ _gen Traum___ Wie ein blas_ser Tropfen Bluts färbt die Lip_pen ei_ner
sf
p

steigernd
Fl.
Kl. (A)
p
cresc.
steigernd
25
Kran - ken.
steigernd
p dolce legato
cresc.
poco rit.
f
nimmt Baß-Klarinette in B
poco rit.
Heiß und jauch - zend, süß und schmach - tend,
poco rit.
ff
sf
p
fpp
ff
ruhiger
pp
B-Kl. (B)
30
ruhiger
me - lan - cho - lisch dü - strer Wal - zer, kommst mir nim - mer aus den
30
ruhiger
pp
sf

Fl.
B-Kl. (B)
Sinnen, haftest mir an den Ge - dan - ken wie ein blas - ser Trop - fen Bluts!
35
40
rit.
44 molto rit.
folgt ohne Pause:
Madonna.
Flöte, Baß-Klarinette in B, Violoncell; später dazu Klavier, Geige.
Segue directly to
"Madonna"

6. Madonna.

┌ ┐ bedeutet Hauptstimme.

Fl.
B-Kl. (B)
Vcl.
arco
G Saite
Sehr ruhig beginnend, nach und nach mächtig steigernd.
mf (ziemlich voll)
In den ab - ge - zehr - ten Hän-den hältst du dei-nes Sohnes Lei-
pizz.
pesante
Tempo
f (immer pizz.)
pesante cresc.
- che, ihn zu zei-gen al-ler Mensch - heit- doch der Blick der Menschen mei-det dich, o
Geige.
wuchtig
Mut - - ter al-ler Schmer - zen!
Klav.
*) hinaufschleifen, während die angerissene Saite weiterklingt.
längere Pause
Der kranke Mond.
Flöte allein.
A lengthy pause before "Der kranke Mond"

7. Der kranke Mond.

II. Teil.

8. Nacht.

(Passacaglia)

B-Kl. (B)
Vcl.
Flatterzunge
am Steg
pp dim.
ppp
cresc.
Tie - fen steigt ein Duft,
Erinnrung mordend!
Fin - stre, schwar - ze
stacc.
cresc.
ohne Ped.
I. Tempo
am Griffbrett
15
Rie - senfal - ter tö - te - ten der Sonne Glanz.
dim.
espress.
Flag.
Und vom Him - mel er - denwärts
sen - ken sich mit schwe - ren Schwin - gen
molto legato

B-Kl. (B)
Vcl.
p dim.
p
dim.
20
un - - sichtbar die Un - - ge - tü - me auf die Men - - schen -
dim.
her - - - zen nie - der...
mf
fin - - stre, schwar - - ze
dim.
8
nimmt Klarinette in A
pp
sf
25
Rie - - sen - fal - - ter.
sehr große Pause, aber quasi im Takt, dann folgt:
Gebet an Pierrot.
Klavier, Klarinette in A.
A very long pause, but practically in tempo, then go on to
"Gebet an Pierrot"

9. Gebet an Pierrot.

Die Rezitation hat die Tonhöhe andeutungsweise zu bringen.

Kl. (A)
frei
Tempo
sf
(10)
Tempo (gesungen)
rot! mein La_chen hab ich ver- -lernt! O
10
Tempo
pp
cresc.
accel.
poco rit.
f
accel. (gesprochen)
(15)
poco rit.
gib mir wie - der, Roß_arzt der See - le, Schnee-
accel.
15
espr.
poco rit.
molto rit.
ppp
molto rit.
pp
(20)
mann der Lyrik, Durchlaucht vom Mon - de, Pi_er_rot - mein La - - chen!
molto rit.
20
stacc.
folgt ohne jede Pause (bloß aushalten):
Raub.
Flöte, Klarinette in A, Geige (mit Dämpfer), Violoncell (mit Dämpfer)
Go on without pause to "Raub"
(merely make the long)

10. Raub.

Mäßige ♩ (ca. 84)
Flöte.
Klarinette in A.
Geige. (mit Dämpfer)
Violoncell. (mit Dämpfer)
Rezitation.
col legno gestrichen
immer col legno gestrichen
mit der Rezitation
arco am Griffbrett flautando
streng im Takt weiter
Ro - te, fürstli-che Ru - bi - ne, blutge Trop-fen al - ten Ruh-mes
schlummern in den To-tenschreinen, drunten in den Grabgewölben.
espress.
arco
am Griffbrett flautando
(tonlos)
Nachts,

Fl.
Kl. (A)
G.
Vcl.
arco am Griffbrett
pizz.
deutlich
arco
(ton)
(tonlos)
(ton etc.
mit seinen Zechkumpanen steigt Pier-rot hin-ab,
zu rau-ben ro-te,
fürst-li-che Ru-bi-ne,
blut-ge Trop-fen al-ten Ruh-mes.
accel.
pizz.
arco am Steg
am Steg
Doch da sträuben sich die Haare,
bleiche Furcht bannt sie am Plat-ze:

accel.
Fl.
Kl. (A)
G.
Vcl.
Flag.
cresc.
durch die Fin-ster-nis, wie Au-gen!- stie - ren aus den To - tenschreinen
molto rit.
pizz.
arco
am Steg
ro - te, fürst-li - che Ru - bi - ne.
nimmt Piccolo
nimmt Baß-Klarinette
nimmt Bratsche
(quasi Adagio) molto rit. (von ♪ ca 80 bis ♪ ca 100-90)
molto stacc.
Klav.
folgt ohne jede Pause:
Rote Messe.
Klavier, Piccolo, Baß-Klarinette in B, Bratsche, Violoncell.
Segue directly to "Rote Messe"

11. Rote Messe.

poco rit.
Pic.
B-Kl. (B)
Br.
Vcl.
am Steg
pizz.
ppp
col legno gestrichen
pppp
tar– Pi - er - rot!
poco rit.
fp
rit.
breiter (langsamer)
sfpp
arco
fff
Die Hand,
martellato
ppp
ff

molto rit.
Tempo
Pic.
B-Kl.
(B)
Br.
Vel.
molto rit.
fff
Tempo
die gott - geweihte, zer - reißt die Prie - ster - klei - der.
molto rit.
Tempo
molto rit.
Tempo I.
Pic.
B-Kl.
(B)
Br.
Vel.
am Steg
am Steg
15
molto rit.
Tempo I.
Zu grau - sem A - bend - mah - le beim Blen - deglanz des
molto rit.
15
Tempo I.
r. H.
l. H.

poco rit. - - Tempo
Pic.
B-Kl. (B)
ppp stacc.
ppp
p
dolce espress.
Br.
ppp stacc.
ppp
p
p
espress.
Vcl.
ppp stacc.
ppp
p
p
espress.
p
20
Gol - des.
Mit seg - nender Geber - - de zeigt er
poco rit. - - Tempo
stumm niederdrücken
Flag.
pp
dolce
pp
20
p
espress.
ohne Ped.
f
immer ohne Ped.
poco rit.
Pic.
B-Kl. (B)
p
am Steg
Br.
p
pp
Vcl.
molto espress.
poco rit.
den ban - gen, ban - - gen See - len, die trie - fend ro - te Ho - stie:
poco rit.
3
pp espress.
bedeutet Hauptstimme.

Tempo
Pic.
B-Kl. (B)
am Steg
Br.
sehr ruhig
Vcl.
am Steg
dim.
Tempo
(gesungen)
25
(gesprochen)
sein Herz in blut - gen Fin - gern zu grau - - - -
25 Tempo
molto rit.
am Griffbrett flautando
Flag.
- sem A - bend - mah - le.
29
äußerst kurze Pause (im Takt) folgt: Galgenlied.
Piccolo.
Bratsche.
Violoncell.
Extremely short pause (in tempo), then go on to "Galgenlied"

12. Galgenlied.

13. Enthauptung.

┌ ┐ bedeutet Hauptstimme.

*) Hier darf keine Stimme hervortreten; bloß die mit „sf" bezeichneten Stellen haben sich deutlich abzuheben.
+) bedeutet: pizz. mit der linken Hand

rit.
Tempo
B-Kl. (B)
Br.
Vcl.
Sei - denkis - sen.
Es schlottern un - ter ihm die Knie,
hervor
accel.
ohn - mächtig bricht er jäh zusammen. Er wähnt: es sause strafend schon auf sei - nen Sündenhals her -
G-Saite
gliss.
20
martellato
nie - der der Mond, das blan - ke Tür - kenschwert.

⌜ ⌝ bedeutet Hauptstimme.

14. Die Kreuze.

Blu - tes Schar - - lach! Heil - - ge Kreu - ze sind die Ver - se, dran die
r. H.
f
cresc.
ten.
ff
accel.
martellato
Dich - - - ter stumm ver - blu - - - - - -
tr
Ped.
Flöte.
pp
Flatterzunge
Klarinette in A.
Geige.
Flag.
Violoncell.
Doppelgriff es u. h.
10
ffpp
(ernst)
- ten. Tot das Haupt, erstarrt die Locken - fern ver -
Flag.
tonlos niederdrücken
l. H.
ppp
✲ ohne Pedal
immer ohne Ped.

Fl.
Kl. (A)
ppp sehr ruhig, ohne Ausdruck
G.
ppp sehr ruhig, ohne Ausdruck
Vcl.
ppp sehr ruhig, ohne Ausdruck
weht der Lärm des Pö - bels. Lang - - - sam sinkt die Son - ne
ppp stacc.
ohne Ped.
spiccato
pizz.
arco
p
cresc.
fp
15
nie - der, ei - ne ro - te Kö - - - nigs - kro - ne.
molto cresc.
molto stacc.
ffp

sehr breit
Fl.
Kl. (A)
G.
Vcl.
Schalltrichter hoch
ff
sehr breit
Heil_ge Kreuze sind die Ver_se.
sehr breit
fff
pp
ffpp
f
20
Schluß des II. Teiles.
End of Part II

III. Teil.

15. Heimweh.

Tempo
etwas zögernd
Kl. (A)
G.
G-Saite
ta - liens al - ter Pan-to - mi - me, klingt's her-ü - ber: wie Pierrot so höl - zern, so mo - dern sen - ti - men - tal
espress.
f molto espress.
D-Saite
poco accel.
ge-wor - den.
Und es tönt durch sei-nes Herzens Wü - ste,
cresc.

Geige: ++ pizz. mit der linken Hand.

Kl. (A)
G.
Da ver - gißt Pier -
Ped.
rot die Trau - - - - - - - - - - - er - mie - nen! Durch den
20
poco rit.
Tempo
steigernd
blei - chen Feu - erschein des Mon - des, durch des Licht - meers Flu - ten schweift die

poco rit.
molto rit.
Kl. (A)
G.
cresc.
fff
Sehn - sucht kühn hin - auf, em - por zum Hei - - - mat - him - mel,
cresc.
ff
Ped.
ppp
Flag.
25 sehr langsam
lieb - lich kla - gend ein kry - stall - - nes Seuf - zen.
arpegg.
tonlos niederdrücken
Flag.
ohne Pedal!
Sehr rasch.
Piccolo.
Violoncell.
rit.
Flag. C-Saite.
folgt ohne Pause:
Gemeinheit.
(Klavier, Piccolo, Klarinette (A) Geige, Violoncell.)
Go on without pause to
"Gemeinheit"

16. Gemeinheit.

Pic.
Kl. (A)
G.
Vcl.
arco
ruhig
(10)
mit dem Daumen seinen ech - - ten türk - - schen
molto rit.
am Steg
(beiseite)
(15)
(im Takt)
Ta - bak in den blan - ken Kopf Cas - san - ders, des - sen Schrei die Luft durchzetert.

Tempo I.
Pic.
Kl. (A)
G.
Vcl.
immer ganzer Bogen
Tempo I.
Dann dreht er ein Rohr von Weich - sel hin - ten
Tempo I.
poco rit.
breiter Auftakt
immer langsamer werdend
pizz.
arco
20
in die glat - te Glat - ze
und be-hag - lich schmaucht und pafft er sei-nen

Pic.
Kl. (A)
G.
Vcl.
ech - ten türk - schen Ta - bak
aus dem blan - ken
pp
rit.
pizz.
nimmt Bratsche
25
Kopf
Cas - san - ders!
große ausgiebige Pause, dann folgt: Parodie.
(Klavier, Piccolo, Klarinette in A, Bratsche.)
A long, extensive pause, then go on to "Parodie"

17. Parodie.

(♪= ca 132)
Piccolo.
Klarinette imitiert genau den Vortrag der Bratsche.
Klarinette in A.
grazioso
mit Dämpfer
Bratsche.
grazioso
p stacc. spicc. springender Bogen
Rezitation.
Strick - - nadeln, blank und
(♪= ca 132)
durchaus begleitend
Klavier.
Pic.
Kl. (A)
Br.
sentimental
p dolce
D-Saite
5
blin - kend, in ih - rem grau - - en Haar, sitzt
espress.
l. H.
dolce

Pic.
Kl. (A)
Br.
ppp subito
die Du-en - na- mur - - - - melnd im ro - ten
legato
pp legato
stacc.
(zögernd)
ppp
Röck - chen da.
Sie wartet in der Lau-be, sie liebt
Pierrot mit Schmer - zen.
cresc.
hervortretend

Pic.
Kl. (A)
Br.
Strick - nadeln, blank und blin - kend, in ih - rem
wieder begleitend
poco dim.
ppp stacc.
marcato
nimmt große Flöte
rit.
grau - en Haar.
20
Etwas langsamer.
Fl.
sehr ruhig
Da plötzlich— horch— ein Wis-pern! ein Windhauch kichert lei - se:
am Steg

Segue directly to
"Der Mondfleck"
attacca

18. Der Mondfleck.

Pic.
Kl. (B)
G.
Vcl.
rot im lauen A_bend,
auf_zu_suchen Glück und A_ben_teu_er.
cresc.
Plötzlich stört ihn was an sei_nem An_zug, er be_

Pic.
Kl. (B)
G.
Vcl.
cresc.
dim.
sieht sich rings und fin_det rich_tig- ei_nen wei_ßen Fleck
des hel_len Mon_ - des auf dem Rük_ken sei_nes schwarzen Rockes. War_te!

Pic.
Kl. (B)
G.
Vcl.
denkt er: das ist so ein Gips - fleck!
Wischt und wischt, doch
15
(ärgerlich)
bringt ihn nicht her- - un - ter!
(erregt)
Und so geht er
15
pp cresc.

Pic.
Kl. (B)
G.
Vcl.
cresc.
f cresc.
cresc.
(komisch bedeutsam)
gift - geschwollen wei-ter, reibt und reibt
bis an den frühen Morgen
ei-nen
hervor
fp
sf
ff
pp
f
wei - - ßen Fleck des hel-len Mon-des.
19
pp
ohne größere Pause, bloß aushalten, folgt:
Serenade.
Klavier, Violoncell
Übergang zu Heimfahrt kommen dazu Flöte, Klarinette in A, Geige.
Without much of a pause, merely holding the , go on to "Serenade"
In the transition to "Heimfahrt" [mm. 46–53], flute, clarinet in A, and violin are added.

19. Serenade.

Sehr langsamer Walzer (mäßige 𝅗𝅥.) ♩= ca 120-132; sehr frei vorzutragen.
Violoncell.
Rezitation.
Klavier.
Sehr langsamer Walzer (mäßige 𝅗𝅥.) ♩= ca 120-132
Sehr langsamer Walzer (mäßige 𝅗𝅥.) ♩= ca 120-132
espress.
p
sf
mf
Vcl.
f
p
pizz.
psf
dolce
espress.
(pizz.)
molto rit.
arco
dolce
pp
Tempo
Mit groteskem

Vcl.
Rie-sen-bo-gen kratzt Pier-rot auf sei-ner Brat-sche. Wie der Storch auf ei-nem Bei-ne
rit.
p
20
knipst er trüb ein Piz-zi-ca-to.
immer p
pp
langsam - accel. - - - - - - rit.
ad libitum
f
Tempo
brillant
25
langsam - accel. - - - - rit.
Tempo
Plötz-lich naht Cas-
rit.
sf
poco rit.
san-der, wü- - tend ob des näch-ti-gen Vir-tuo- - sen.
cresc.
poco rit.

ruhiger
Vcl.
(ruhig)
Mit gro-tes--kem Rie--sen-bo--gen kratzt
ruhiger
Pier-rot auf sei-ner Brat-sche.
(breit)
frei
Tempo
brillant
rit.
C-Saite
dolce
Tempo
Von sich wirft er jetzt die Brat-sche: mit der de-li-ka-ten Linken
poco string.
rit.
Tempo
fließend
faßt er den Kahl-kopf am Kra-gen—
träu--mend spielt
cresc.

Without pause, move immediately into **"Heimfahrt"**

20. Heimfahrt.

(Barcarole)

poco rit.
Fl.
Kl. (A)
G.
Vcl.
arco
arco
ppp
poco rit.
Der Mond - - strahl ist das Ru - - - der,
poco rit.
pp
poco espress.
Tempo
espress.
p
espress.
p
p
p
See - ro - se dient als Boot,
Tempo

Fl.
Kl. (A)
G.
Vcl.
Flatterzunge
pizz.
arco
10
drauf fährt Pier - rot gen Sü - - den mit gu - - tem Rei - se - wind.
Der Strom summt tie - fe Ska - len und wiegt

poco rit.
Flatterzunge.
Fl.
pp
Kl. (A)
pp
dolce
G.
pp
dolce
Vcl.
pp
dolce
poco rit.
15
— den leich - ten Kahn.
Der Mond - strahl ist das Ru - der,
poco rit.
15
sfpp
espress.
Tempo
Flatterzunge.
Fl.
pp
Kl. (A)
G.
spiccato
spiccato
spiccato
Vcl.
spiccato
spiccato
Tempo
See - ro - se dient als Boot.
Tempo

Fl.
Kl. (A)
G.
Vcl.
p espress.
p dolce
p
Nach Ber-ga-mo, zur Heimat, kehrt nun Pier-rot zurück;
espress.
pp
pizz.
tr
20
schwach däm - mert schon im O - sten der grü - - ne Ho - ri - zont.

Flatterzunge.
Fl.
Kl. (A)
G.
Vel.
arco
pizz.
pp
Der Mond - strahl ist das Ru - der.
sfpp
25
sf
Dämpfer weg!
30
folgt: (ohne Pause!) „O alter Duft."
Klavier, Flöte (Piccolo), Klarinette (Baß-Klar.), Geige (Bratsche), Violoncell.
Segue (without pause!) to "O alter Duft"

21. O alter Duft.

poco rit.
Tempo
rit.
Tempo
Fl.
Kl. (A)
nimmt Baß Klarinette in B
G.
nimmt Bratsche
Vcl.
poco rit.
Tempo
rit.
Tempo
sehr innig
Wünschen macht mich froh nach Freu - den, die ich lang ver - ach - - tet. O
p
poco rit.
p espress.
Tempo
rit.
p
Tempo
poco rit.
Tempo
Fl.
Baß-Klarinette (B)
Bratsche.
Vcl.
p espress.
15
poco rit.
Tempo
al - ter Duft aus Mär - chen - zeit, be - rau - schest wie - der mich. All meinen
poco rit.
ppp
Tempo

Fl.
B-Kl. (B)
Br.
Vcl.
nimmt Piccolo
Un-mut geb ich preis; aus meinem sonnumrahm-ten Fenster beschau ich frei die lie-be Welt und
Piccolo.
rit.
Tempo
molto rit.
B-Kl. (B.)
Dämpfer aufsetzen
mit Dämpfer
träum hin-aus in sel-ge Weiten... O al-ter Duft aus Mär-chen-zeit!

THE END